FIVE TASTES

FIVE TASTES

PROSE POEMS BY

Cassandra Atherton

Oz Hardwick

Paul Hetherington

Paul Munden

Jen Webb

authorised theft

☆ ◎ ✺ ✤ ☀

FIVE TASTES

authorised theft / Recent Work Press

Canberra, Australia

This chapbook series was produced with the support of International Poetry Studies (IPSI), based within the Centre for Creative and Cultural Research, Faculty of Arts and Design, University of Canberra.

http://ipsi.org.au

Collection © Recent Work Press 2022

The copyright of the individual poems remains with the authors.

ISBN 978-0-6456512-0-1

Design: Caren Florance

Cover image by Caren Florance, using 'HellMouth', from p.78 of the British Library's digitisation of *Cassell's Library of English Literature. Selected, edited and arranged by H. M. ... Illustrated*, found in The Commons on Flickr.com

recentworkpress.com

RECENT
WORK
PRESS

CONTENTS

The AUTHORISED THEFT series of poetry chapbooks was initiated by International Poetry Studies (IPSI) based in the Faculty of Arts and Design at the University of Canberra. The frst collection of chapbooks—Cassandra Atherton's Pegs, *Paul Hetherington's* Jars, *Paul Munden's* Keys, *Jen Webb's* Gaps *and Jordan Williams'* Nets—*resulted from discussions connected to IPSI's Prose Poetry Project, inaugurated by IPSI in late 2014. A second collection,* The Taoist Elements, *followed in 2016; a third,* Colours, *in 2017; and a fourth,* Prosody, *in 2018. A fifth series,* The Six Senses, *followed in anthology form in 2019 and, in 2020, the sixth collection, also in anthology form, was entitled* C19: Intertext || Ekphrasis. *The 2021 anthology,* Five Ages, *took Hesiod's conceptualisation of human history as its starting point, including Oz Hardwick as a new contributing author, while, in 2022, the anthology focuses on the five tastes. IPSI supports and promotes collaborative and collegiate poetic work in a variety of forms, and encourages the collaboration of poets with other artists, such as Caren Florance who has designed the series.*

TASTING THE WORLD

Paul Hetherington

THIS EIGHTH COLLECTION of *Authorised Theft* chapbooks continues the broadly collaborative series (now consolidated into an annual anthology) featuring 21 prose poems by each of five prose poets per year. The chapbook series began in 2015 as five small, standalone publications containing the work of Cassandra Atherton, Paul Hetherington, Paul Munden, Jen Webb and Jordan Williams. In 2021 Oz Hardwick became part of the group after Jordan Williams left. In 2022, each member has written prose poems focused broadly on one of the five main tastes—bitter, salty, sour, sweet, and umami.

Unsurprisingly, many of these prose poems are about eating and tasting. However, a wide variety are also about other subjects, exploring how frequently language uses concepts related to taste in metaphorical ways. Carmen Maria Bretones Callejas writes that '[r]ecent work in metaphorical analysis makes it clear that many of our most basic concepts (and our reasoning via those concepts) are embodied' (2001, 3). She continues, '[o]ne of the most common types of metaphoric transfer is synaesthesia ... i.e., the transfer of information from one sensory modality to another' (4). She proceeds to analyse a selection of Seamus Heaney's 'synaesthetic metaphors', including those where 'tasting is touching', 'touching is tasting' and 'hearing is tasting'. An example she gives is the phrase, 'I savoured the rich crash' (qtd. in Callejas 2001, 15).

If metaphors often cross over between the senses of taste, touch, smell, hearing and sight—and even the sixth sense— metaphors drawn from taste also relate to numerous other domains, including aesthetic judgement. For instance, it is fairly commonplace to refer to a person's good or bad 'taste' in clothes, shoes, art, and diverse other matters. In such instances, the notion of taste, instead of being directly connected to eating, becomes a quality possessed by an individual or group that refers to human judgement, experience, social position and status. Pierre Bourdieu discusses such matters at length in *Distinction: A Social Critique of the Judgement of Taste*, remarking that:

> cultural needs are the product of upbringing and education . . . [and] all cultural practices (museum visits, concert-going, reading etc.), and preferences in literature, painting or music, are closely linked to educational level (measured by qualifications or length of schooling) and secondarily to social origin . . . This predisposes tastes to function as markers of 'class'. (2000, 1–2)

Ivy Ken draws on Bourdieu's ideas in considering 'the parallels between the production of food and the production of race, class, and gender' (2010, 7). She observes that 'A food product becomes a flavor when a person experiences it, and people are likely to experience it differently' (9). Nicola Perullo states:

> Taste is both pleasure and knowledge; in some cases what's good is only related to pleasure, but in others, it is only related to knowledge; more often than not, it is related to both taken together. So 'good' refers to a grammar of values where social and cultural codes claim as much space as instinct and personal experience do. (2016, xi)

The prose poets in this volume explore such issues, aware that the five tastes come in an almost endless variety, and that the concepts of good or bad taste are frequently problematic.

The smell, texture and pungency of food also influence the way it is 'tasted'. In *The Physiology of Taste*, originally published in France in 1825, Jean Anthelme Brillat-Saverin observes that: 'there exists an indefinite series of simple tastes which can change according to the number and variety of their combinations, [and] we should need a whole new language to describe all these effects' (2009, 48). He adds:

> Up to the present time there is not a single circumstance in which a given taste has been analyzed with stern exactitude, so we have been forced to depend on a small number of generalizations such as sweet, sugary, sour, bitter and other like ones which express, in the end, no more than the words *agreeable* and *disagreeable*, and are enough … to indicate, more or less, the taste properties of the sapid body which they describe. (48)

In the prose poems that follow, the five tastes are understood in sensual and intellectual terms; in explorations of diverse experiences; as metaphorical figurations; as social and political constructions; as ways of commenting on bodily knowledge; as literary tropes and intertextual prompts; and also, of course, as what we may experience when preparing and eating food. There are innumerable ways of 'tasting' and apprehending the world, and these poems canvass a wide range of them while also encouraging readers to consider their own diverse tastes, preferences and experiences.

Works Cited

Bourdieu, Pierre 2000 *Distinction: A Social Critique of the Judgement of Taste*, translated by Richard Nice, Cambridge, MA: Harvard University Press

Brillat-Savarin, Jean Anthelme 2009 *The Physiology of Taste; or, Meditations on Transcendental Gastronomy*, translated and edited by M.F.K. Fisher, New York, NY: Alfred A. Knopf

Callejas, Carmen Maria Bretones 2001 'Synaesthetic Metaphors in English', ftp://ftp.icsi.berkeley.edu/pub/techreports/2001/tr-01-008.pdf, 1–23

Ken, Ivy 2010 *Digesting Race, Class, and Gender: Sugar as a Metaphor*, New York, NY: Palgrave Macmillan

Perullo, Nicola 2016 *Taste as Experience: The Philosophy and Aesthetics of Food*, New York, NY: Columbia University Press

RESEARCH STATEMENT

TASTING, THINKING, BEING

Jen Webb

Bitter, salty, sour, sweet, and umami: the five tastes remind us, with everything that passes our lips, that we are part of the animal kingdom, part of the natural as well as the cultural world. Like all other living beings, we know the world in no small part through the sensation of how things feel in our mouth, how they taste on our tongue. Taste is (almost) universal, but is also highly individualised, based both on what Aristotle terms 'habituation' (1869, 22) and on an individual's physiological make-up. How many taste buds do you have on your tongue? To which of the five tastes are they more closely attuned? For supertasters, people born with more than the average taste buds and receptors, flavours are more vibrant, bitterness more intense. For those with fewer than average taste buds and receptors, flavour is less vibrant, bitterness no more intense than is sweet or sour or salty (see Li, Streletskaya & Gómez 2019).

The multiple experiences of taste and taste sensitivity, and the ambiguity of the way the term 'taste' is used, parallel the structure and the slipperiness of the word itself. Taste is a homonym, after all, one that bears many possible meanings and functions. It does double duty as verb and noun. In its verb form, it can operate as transitive ('I can taste the difference') and as intransitive ('That food tastes sour'). And, in its noun form, it carries a basketful of connotative and denotative meanings, including flavour, sensation, consumption, experience, emotion, preference, perception, discernment, testing, *et al*. Taste is not easily pinned down.

In the long record of philosophical writing, taste emerges primarily as a concept, a tool for discrimination. We see this in terms of both physical and social organisation in Aristotle's *Ethics*, where he notes 'To the taste properly belongs the distinction of flavours', and then notes rather loftily that the temperate and the trained actually understand the quality of flavours, while flavour as such doesn't matter to 'the intemperate', for whom 'venery' and acts of gluttony provide their pleasures (Aristotle 1869, 93). It's pretty clear who are the more 'magnificent' and who are the lowlife he terms 'cormorants'—which, he explains, means the 'belly-mad' (95). Sophisticated people, people of reason, eat only what they need, and are also capable of distinguishing tastes, taking pleasure in quality rather than quantity.

David Hume, writing some two millennia after Aristotle, takes a similar perspective when he maps out the modes of moral philosophy. These, he argues, are split between two perspectives: the first that humans are creatures of action, motivated 'by taste and sentiment'; the second that humans are creatures of reason, motivated by the hunger to understand (2000, 5). The latter is clearly his preferred option, and this parallels Descartes' mind-body dualism, where mind is what is valued, what makes us human, while body with all its needs and demands is mere flesh.

The prose poems in this volume offer a range of representations and evocations of the five different tastes, and the many meanings of the word 'taste', from the perspective of five different poets, and across 105 poems. What we hope this conveys is the fluidity and plurality of experience and perception, the capacity of poeisis to draw out potential meanings and sensations, and the recognition that humans may have the property of abstraction and idealism, but are also always deeply embedded in the world. Because, as poet Antjie Krog writes, 'the action of eating, of taking in food is simply enchanting—because it's the way we can take up the world inside ourselves, how what is around us becomes part of us. We eat the world' (Krog 1998, 217). And, in that process of eating, and the choices we make of what to take in, how much to take in, how to think about that process, we can engage more thoughtfully with the world of which we are one small part.

Works Cited

Aristotle 1869 [c.350BCE] *Nicomachean Ethics*, translated by Robert Williams, London: Spottiswoods and Co

Descartes, René 1968 [1637] *Discourse on Methods and the Meditations*, translated by F.E. Sutcliffe, Harmondsworth: Penguin

Hume, David 2000 [1748] *An Enquiry Concerning Human Understanding*, edited by Tom Beauchamp, Oxford: Oxford University Press

Krog, Antjie 1998 *Country of My Skull*, London: Random House

Li, Jie, Nadia A. Streletskaya and Miguel I. Gómez 2019 'Does Taste Sensitivity Matter? The Effect of Coffee Sensory Tasting Information and Taste Sensitivity on Consumer Preferences', *Food Quality and Preference* 71, 447–51

SALTY

CASSANDRA ATHERTON

'Trust no one unless you have eaten much salt with him'
—Marcus Tullius Cicero

'The cure for anything is salt water: sweat, tears or the sea'
—Karen Blixen

TEAR

Time creeps over my body with stealthy, clammy fingers. I writhe, not wanting to feel its long hands marking my bones. You love clocks, wonder at the inner mechanics of a watch, contemplate cogs that fit and turn, and fit again. I remember when we climbed Bath Abbey's wooden stairs, sitting behind the clock-face in the tower. For a moment, you controlled time; for a second you were inside it. Now, I lie in the darkness in a hospital bed, contemplating what I'm willing and unwilling to relinquish. In the mauve light of the digital clock, there is a long tear track from eye to chin. One part of me sleeps, the other wakes. You misread 'tear' and it rips me out of teleology.

CURED 1

Your backpack rests low against my spine. You adjust the straps across my shoulders, pulling the pack up and snapping the toggle that rests across my chest. The deli at *Dem Supermercati* is pink with rounds of meat piled on shelves. You ask for San Daniele prosciutto and the butcher slices a leg of meat, gathering each slice carefully as it floats from the machine to his palm. We buy tinned tuna, bottles of acqua frizzante, shiny green olives in jars and heart-shaped strawberries in punnets. At the cash register you pack everything into the backpack; weighty items first and lighter ones on top. A woman in the queue smiles as I do a little jig to show you it isn't too heavy. When we arrive at our hotel room, you un-toggle me and slide off the pack and then my dress. As I lie on the bed, you remember your prosciutto and, half naked, place it in the fridge. Later when you open the package, the transparent cerise slices are thinner than the waxed paper it's wrapped in.

CURED 2

In the museum shop at the *Thyssen-Bornemisza*, he buys me a Balenciaga filigree choker, its bright blue velvet ribbon threaded through the latticed design. It reminds me of roses growing up a trellis or the unfurling of a music box scroll, with raised notes like braille. When he takes me to dinner, I wear my yellow dress, the accordion pleats reminding him of an origami sun's rays. We revel in the menu's description of mojama: *loins of tuna, cured in salt, washed, laid out to dry in the sun and breeze for 15–20 days*. When it arrives, bright almonds stud the plate and olive oil washes it with light. My thighs quiver when he smooths out a pleat on my skirt. The fanning of salt-cured tuna is like tongues claiming my neck.

OLIVES 1

You feed me green olives like grapes, their oily skins embalming my tongue as I press them against the roof of my mouth and sip their juice. Sometimes you fill my mouth with olives stuffed with sundried tomatoes, roasted garlic cloves or anchovies, but mostly they are pitted, with holes in their tops and small crosses on their bases. Hollow olives; fleshy but no seed in their bellies.

* *

As we sit in the hotel restaurant, I grab an olive from the tiny tapas dish and hold it up to my eye, looking into the olive abyss. 'Are you having an existential moment?' you laugh, drinking your gin and tonic.

* *

You ask me to chop black olives to garnish our pasta bake. I cut them around their girth; little hemispheres tumbling around my wooden chopping board. 'Why didn't you cut them down the middle?' I shrug, watching the slick halves search for ways to sit on their severed ends as you set the timer and unzip the back of my dress.

OLIVES 2

He prods the green olives with a toothpick. I like martinis with three olives but the third one won't quite fit on the end of the stick. He tries to spear it with the small point, squashes it against the wall of glass but it drops away, its pimento like a spinning red flag. Finally, he reaches in and takes it between his fingers. 'Take a swig from the cocktail shaker and then open your mouth.' He drops the third olive into the pool of gin and vermouth. It bobs until I crush it between my back teeth. I peel him a piece of rind from the lemon in the fruit bowl and he twists it into a corkscrew shape. I pull the second olive from the toothpick.

UMEBOSHI 1

Our icebox is full of gin and the fridge chills a dozen bottles of Billecart Salmon. I take an onigiri from the crisper, a salty plum at its centre, like a misshapen heart.

* *

You suck out the umeboshi from the middle of my rice ball and pour champagne.

* *

We wake to a Tokyo blue sky. The clock tower lights up red and green and casts its light over our naked bodies. As you pull me under you, I feel the spaces between my ribs narrow.

UMEBOSHI 2

He holds my hand when Mion sings the cherry blossom lullaby. She strums the three strings of the sanshin, the scales of its snakeskin body waxy under her palm. He orders stir-fried bitter melon with egg and tofu while I have rice porridge. The melon rind is tart and shaped like a green cog. I watch him taste the saffron threads and push them aside. My okayu has a pickled plum in the centre, like the Japanese flag. As she sings the high-pitched notes, he promises to take me to Okinawa. I pick up the wrinkled fruit in my chopsticks as he waves his arms out of time to the music.

SWEAT 1

Your shirt is wet and the hairs on your arms stick to my skin in long straight lines, like em dashes. You tell me you've wheeled your case several blocks but the stickiness of your sweat, its gluey toxicity, surely indicates Covid fever. You fill my hesitation with desire and I slide from the curve of my question mark to its full stop. In a thick scent of raisin toast and melting butter, you kiss my earlobe and say I'm your raison d'être. Before I can express my preference for sultanas, you fit yourself inside me, your skin's flush lighting up my collarbone.

SWEAT 2

I leave a ring of salt on his car seat. Not a magic circle to protect passengers or ward off bad luck, just an outline, where my buttocks connected with the black pleather on the hot drive home.

TABLE SALT 1

At breakfast, you balance tuna and chopped tomato on a piece of wholegrain toast. I reach for a slice of the red sockeye smoked salmon to eat with some avocado and knock over the saltshaker. A strip of white crystals stretches across the tablecloth like sand escaping from an hourglass. I gather grains between my thumb and forefinger but I don't know which shoulder to throw it over. 'What was Lot's wife's name?' I ask. The tuna and tomato tower wobbles before it falls in pieces into your open palm.

TABLE SALT 2

I shake salt over a teacup of warm water. Stirring with my finger, I push the stray grains that sit on the bottom until they dissolve. I ask him to dip a corner of the flannel into the cup while I pick up our cat. His tail moves in strange 's' shapes across my arm as I pat the wet towel over his red eye. When I release him, he leaps onto the bench and, one eye closed, knocks the cup onto the floor. I dab at the solution with the other side of the flannel, but in the morning sun, the white outline of the stain begins to curl.

BATH 1

As it fizzes and spins in the coloured water, we toast the bath bomb's final Catherine wheel into pinks and blues. I turn on the spa's jets. We have a bubble-on-bubble experience. You say it's an afternoon of double double toil and trouble, lifting the champagne bottle from the ice bucket.

When we let out the water I feel your cold hands on my hot buttocks, as you peel off my bikini bottoms and edge your knee between my thighs. You say my body is a cauldron.

BATH 2

He shakes bath salts into the running water while I sit with a hot towel over my face. He turns off the tap and when the water is still, I peel off the towel and open my eyes. Turquoise and green water—he has given me the Seto Inland Sea.

OYSTERS 1

In lockdown you shucked oysters with me—dozens and dozens in bright netted bags. Easing the oysters' hinges and sliding the knife between the clamped edges of the shell, we felt the suction and release of the bivalve like an exhalation.

* *

My favourite oyster shells are crescent-shaped, their sharp, pointed tips like a sickle moon. You prefer smooth oval shells with frills at their edges like a bed valance. The first time we ate oysters together I cried because you didn't believe in anything after death and I couldn't imagine the end of our shared time. As I encouraged an oyster into my mouth, you picked up its shell and drank the briny liquor.

OYSTERS 2

He wanted to unpack the car—five trips with boxes and bags. He propped the heaviest box on the handrail in the lift while I carried the esky full of unshucked oysters. He said we should turn down the temperature in the fridge, chill the champagne, pour water into the ice trays and unpack the groceries. And then he looked for power points and plugged in his phone. As I stowed my suitcase against the wall, I remembered the days when we barely made it from the lift to the door, his arms around my waist, fingers climbing my thigh.

OCEAN 1

Feet first, we descend into sky-blue water, my hair a thick plaited crown. Sitting on barnacles and seaweed, the waves crash over the barrier chains in a canon of salt and light. While I'm pushed up against the rocks, you wash over me with the curling sea foam. For a moment, we are a haunting of contiguous limbs, a mingling of flesh and bone. Over our shoulders, wind-driven waves roll against the grey sky.

OCEAN 2

I hid the orange inflatable boat under my bed, hoping my childhood might sail into my dreams—sunny afternoons with soggy Savoy crackers disintegrating on the boat's bottom, large chunks of Kraft cheese floating in an inch of salty water that rose from a slow leak somewhere in the plastic. It was a moving waterbed—nana in her purple butterfly bathers taking the white plastic rope, leading me over water from pier to boat ramp until I was asleep.

SALTED CARAMEL 1

In Madrid's heatwave, my washed hair dries in ten minutes as we walk to the *Supermercado El Corte Inglés*. I say my orange hair is fluffed up with sun but you say it's like a halo from Simone Martini's *Annunciation*. The square in front of the Opera House is as bleached as an old photo in sepia and cream. We stop to buy gelato. You choose nocciola and invite me to taste its nutty sweetness. I run my tongue around the edge of the cone. My gelato melts and streaks of caramel run on the back of my hand. A group of street musicians begins to play Pachelbel's *Canon*. The violin is mournful, cycling through brackish and honeyed notes.

SALTED CARAMEL 2

He loves steamed puddings—sticky and sweet with thin ribbons of cream running over the moist mound of cake. He likes every available flavour except for salted caramel. He makes a list of foods with salted caramel flavours: doughnuts, popcorn, martinis, cupcakes. He adds to it daily: cheesecake, hot cross buns, ice-cream.

* *

I work the tension from his shoulders with my thumbs and slide my hand down his spine. He reciprocates, kissing me until I'm drunk on lips and tongue. I open the honey-coloured bottle and pour some of the liquid into the little hollows on either side of his back. He tenses when his skin begins to warm under my fingers. 'Stay there,' I tell him, 'I'll add it to the list.'

ANGER 1

There's a certain way she inveigles herself between us at dinner—turning her back, laughing into your ear, clutching at your shirt—that leaves me at the corner of the table to make the smallest of talk. When she bows her head in hushed conversation, I hear the sounds of your consonant replies, whistling through the whispers. She feeds you a piece of meat from her plate, blood running into the green beans, pinking the white china. You say it's juicy and she offers you more, while I drink double vodka sodas and poke my poached salmon with a fork.

* *

I'm firebrand angry, flame driven. You're naked in bed as I stand at its base. We argue, our voices an ugly twisting of words. Until, in white hot silence, we have sex. The rhythmic noise fills the space. We are flesh and breath, two bodies searching for an endpoint.

ANGER 2

The mussels at the pub were large, their open shells poking out of the top of the shiny pot. As we ate, he said we should recite 'our mussel memories'—all you can eat in Bath; three different sauces from the caravan in the Victoria Market; soaking up the chilli flavours with bread slices in South Melbourne; the perfect mussels at a Japanese restaurant in Sydney. We were covered in sauce and juice, our tongues wild with garlic. I offered him the final mollusc.

* *

After lunch, we played seventeen games of pool. He refused to let me win, even the last game. As he potted the black, the noise of balls colliding mimicked the clacking of that last empty mussel shell on his plate.

UMAMI

OZ HARDWICK

*'The world is
not with us enough.
O taste and see'*
—Denise Levertov

TIMESLIP CANTICLE

It's 1908 and my grandmother's learning to knit, an uneven chain of blue loops growing in her lap. I am at the basin, washing glass animals in thin suds, then drying them on an Empire flag. Low sun catches us all through the kitchen window, and we briefly shine like votive lights on the shrine of Our Lady of Temporal Anomalies, before it's 1967. Grandma and the Glass Animals are still playing the pubs and working men's clubs in northern towns, but ditching soul standards for a new groove, emptying small halls with distorted waves. It's 3 a.m. on an unlit road as their Day-Glo bread van drifts into 2023 and animals are fragile as glass. My grandmother knits perfect squares, humming a song that was never played on the radio, while I am at the basin, my throat wadded with blue wool, rinsing the soot from old northern towns until the light retires like a jilted empire.

GOOD NEWS

I woke up with a fresh religion prickling beneath my skin, in which all sins are of the flesh and all blessings are in disguise. Here comes Grace in dogskin, snapping at the Sun like a tossed bone. And there's Patience, straw hat shading their eyes, sketching a retro Heaven in soft pencils. There's been a rough road of doubt and splatter-porn martyrdoms, but now there's Love, like a sober Jim Morrison helping a weary old soldier with his weekly shopping. Our hymns are songs we loved at school, chance rhythms, and football chants without the fucks and fighting talk. Our prayers are the quick crosswords in the free papers. There are simple formulae for conversion printed on train tickets that guards will never check. The blood of our God comes in branded glasses with a reassuring logo (*insert personal preference*) and tastes of forgiveness; their body is more ambiguous but has your name running right through it.

SCENES FROM A MAKESHIFT ORPHANAGE

At the riptide of my tongue, I taste rice and rust. I've taken advice on trust for too long to turn back now, but even I baulk when the doctor claims that the best source of iron is to nail yourself across bomb-impacted windows. She looks sincere and her voice is that of a satisfying meal at the end of a demanding day, but her white coat is suspiciously stained and when I ask what kind of doctor she is, she just hums the choruses from *Oliver!* A hospital is not a hotel, though the opposite is not always true, and when the windows blow in, we're all hooked into the *drip drip drip* of facts and their duplicitous twins, handing out red and blue pills which taste of rice and rust. The doctor whets the edge of her tongue and I can sense the approaching flood and famine which inevitably follow plague and siege in the beleaguered city. Outside the window is an oven but our plates are empty but for broken glass. The doctor prescribes a turn of the tide but regrets that the waiting list may be longer than the average life expectancy in such predictably unpredictable circumstances. In the meantime, I should take the pills, hold my tongue, hold my breath, and consider myself one of the family. *We don't want to have no fuss*, she smiles, steadying the point of a rusty nail at the dead centre of my palm.

THE MALTRAVIESO EFFECT

Before Eden, before serpents and excuses, even before fruit trees, we were nothing but paint on stone. Our meaningless speech was paint, our aimless actions were paint, and our desires, too, with all their overwhelming innocence, were paint. The only sound I remember is pigment-moistened fingers teasing light from darkness, self from not-self; a sound nearer to music than to God, a sound like passing asteroids in the Kuiper Belt, a sound like forgetting your own heartbeat. Colours were different then. Sure, there was black and white, but in between were harmonics and umami, the precise shades of wonder and falling asleep. Sometimes we were more paint, sometimes more stone, but the point at which they touched was precisely 20ºC and nurtured the seeds of trees and serpents.

TRACKER

You're wrapped in colours, a riot of tape and tongues, stimulating the sensation range of a puppy—pleasant only within relatively narrow concentrations—an aftertaste associated with salivation or furriness of the mouth. You live in the roof by yourself. You wish your mind was mild but all you have are mistakes and ghosts that give no returns—no returns—and there's a lasting aftertaste associated with salivation and the present. This makes a great variety of foods pleasant, especially in the mouth. You live in the present by yourself, by the mouth of a river or a puppy that makes everything palatable but the past. It is pleasant that there are no returns, especially on the tongue which is taped to the roof like a riot of ghosts and fur. Like other basic tastes—mistakes associated with salvation and furrowing of the brows—ribbons retain a lasting aroma, like a puppy yapping at the roof.

ARRIVALS AND DEPARTURES

Planes land on the roof with the thump of pneumatic tyres and that familiar uncertain shuffling. In a while, the house will fill with tourists, rubber rings circling slim midriffs, blinking behind shades. For now, though, we can take it easy, chat about the war over strong black coffee, then line up bird skulls and owl pellets on their specially-made racks. I wonder if owls taste anything as their prey is swallowed and then, later, makes that short journey from gizzard to proventriculus; and I wonder at what point the vole, fieldmouse, or lizard resigns itself to the fact that nothing will ever make sense in the way that it had always hoped it would. Up on the tiles, passengers disembark, holding hands against the treacherous pitch, though I know they'll be fine—they always are. Later, we'll need to check passports, visas, work permits, and biometric data, but there's no rush and for now we can just enjoy the soft light on beaks and bones, the way it plays on fur and feathers. Planes take off and we can feel the house breathe a little lighter. There is more shuffling to the music of recorded announcements. All doors are open. Welcome.

THE DREAM KITCHEN

The dream kitchen carries the tenor, timbre and tremor of a boy's tuneless singing, the tastes that stick for years at the back of the tongue. The cupboards are bare but were designed that way and the induction hobs remain cold to the touch at 260°. The freezer's sufficiently spacious for a nuclear family to sit out a nuclear winter. There are appliances for activities that no one will ever undertake but most importantly there are knives. There are knives at the heart of the design concept, knives at the heart of the family, and knives at the heart of the boy's tuneless song, as he sings for his supper that will never arrive and sings for his mother who's far away, lost on the supermarket sea. We'll dream a new kitchen to hold his hurt, with marble surfaces and new sash windows. Then, we'll dream another, then another, then another, as his hungry tongue trembles at the inexplicable edge of melody.

A PSYCHOGEOGRAPHY OF GOODBYE KISSES

Out on the edgelands, stunted saplings have their own music, rhythmic as an auctioneer's gavel, with the twists and syncopations of a phone call about an unexpected death. To learn it is murder and just to listen is to feel the pull of houses slowly emptying of everything but cladophora-covered curios bought on seaside holidays. There are owls fashioned from common cockle with googly eyes and breath like roadkill, and slipper limpets with broken thermometers and the names of sunken kingdoms etched into their buff curves. The only maps are folded napkins printed with *Flags of the World*, and the only compass is a rusted needle in a broken phone box. Messages have become suspicious, with shopping lists and birthday cards acquiring the aspects of code, while texts and Tweets wear dark glasses even in the noonday sun. Here there are piano keys that drop like fruit from drooping branches. They never play the same note twice and, when you bite into their ivory skin, you're awash with the taste of wind-up gramophones playing a tune that doesn't have a name yet.

I CAN'T BELIEVE IT'S NOT MEMORY

People disappear every day, leaving nothing but blindfold taste tests and indentations in soft furnishing. Occurrences tend to be clustered at points where once were phone boxes and are now small squares of scrub which act as magnets for stray dogs and squalling kids, though correlation may be merely coincidental. Most are forgotten quicker than a child's knees are dabbed with salve, though some are recalled like phone numbers you never had the courage to call. In the future, there will probably be a folk tale trope in which the Princess will marry whoever's head nestles perfectly into the pillow, or whoever's backside is the exact match for the tea-stained La-Z-Boy. In the here and now, though, one can only tie the sash tightly around one's eyes and savour the taste of unremarkable words which were uttered way back before the callbox coins ran out.

STILL LIFE WITH IMPLIED NARRATIVE

The man on the platform thinks about stopping, considers stepping into the pillow of buffeted air, and weighs up the pros and cons of a new career as a solemn warning. Meanwhile, the woman in the window anticipates falling, considers calling the emergency helpline, and resolves once again to rise in inverse proportion to diminishing expectations. Commuters turn away, their unfinished crosswords flapping like white flags in a dirty war, as the express rushes through, bellowing like a mortally wounded bull. Meanwhile, a four-year-old boy in a tiny policeman's uniform fingers the margins of negative space, licks his lips, and tastes the weight of everything for which he doesn't yet have a name.

CRACKED

Fingers in the bowl and eyes dripping with black tea: it's a meal for the melancholy, a moment wiped out by a white napkin, a wedding feast on an erupting volcano, and hungry tongues tasting nothing but ash. There's a cash bar for china webbed with cracks: political smiles smeared across chipped plates, dates pitted against superior odds, and a hot knife translating oil into dreams. There are lies to eat in the dark, initials pricked in fat with steel, bones picked clean of flesh, and fresh blood in the split bowl of fingers. Eyes are bigger than bellies, stewed in the juice of ingredients erased from taboo takeaways and slapped onto a grey slab. The kitchen twitches like spice on sensitive skin. It's thin comfort, but not one of the fingers snapping in the knackered, lacquered bowl has ever belonged to me.

THE ESSENTIALS

Tongues hum like thunder, budding and rippling as they dip, flip, and trip over themselves in search of lightning. Temperate zones. Moist mucosa. Music from the mountains drums a rum rhythm. Debris adrift on a Mexican wave. A skinful of butterflies. Microvilli gossip like whispering grass, their crossed messages careless but insistent. Accidents activate with the force of storms and taste is a grudging trudge from here to the edge of the indescribable. We think, therefore we are bound up in weather, whether we like it or not. A question of imbalance: who goes there? Our brains may tell us we're satisfied but our brains often lie.

THE NEWSPRINT CONNOISSEUR

I miss drawers lined with newspaper and their glimpses of yellowed beach huts and bicycles, their waves of headlines pounding at the edge of forgetfulness until hotels slipped into the sea. One year—I'd have been five or seven because I only lived in odd numbers—I dropped an old threepenny bit in the garden and it grew into a blue metallic tree with fruit like hollow chocolate eggs. It made the local paper but when I saw my name I wasn't sure who they were talking about; and when I saw the picture, my parents looked like film stars and my sister was wrapped in a blanket of stardust, though I had been switched for a turnip in an ill-fitting checked shirt. I wanted to burn every copy but my grandmother kept a clipping in her pocket Bible, slipped into Isaiah 43: *Forget the former things; do not dwell on the past.* I don't know what happened to her Bible, any more than I know what happened to that wonderful tree, but sometimes at Christmas or Easter, or on visits to quaint Belgian cities, I'll allow chocolate to dissolve slowly on my tongue—say five or seven minutes because … well, you know—and it will taste exactly like a drawer lined with newspaper.

A TASTY WORLD

Almost the truth will have to do: the wedding ring that doesn't fit and the facts that leave jagged little gaps. What's that oozing through? Fire, water, earth, or air? Or is it the hand of a crude homunculus, stretching towards someone else's idea of light? Each finger bears a ring: one from a Moroccan market stall, one from a lost mother and her mother before, one from a coin machine in a seaside arcade, and one from a dead soldier's wedding. His smooth sucked thumb tastes of all their broad histories and assumed details, and he offers it to you as if it was a greengage plucked from the air beneath a French sky that is irrevocably lacking in trees. By the time he grows teeth and a tongue of his own, his account will differ wildly from yours or anyone else's. There will be a few elemental facts and a wedding ring cast from clouds, and there will be jagged little gaps full of undeniable sky, but no one will ever agree what the truth tasted like as it oozed through the air like a finger, like a fist, like a figment of a twisted imagination.

THOUGHTS OF THE AVERAGE BEAR

Hungry in the snow, I turn into a bear, pieced together from the half-remembered cartoons that they used to show on the last day of term. I've a pair of patched dungarees, a hat pricked with fishing flies, and a mouth to get me in and out of trouble. I meet an old man with a line through a hole in the ice who doesn't notice that I'm a bear. I meet a park ranger who knows that I'm a bear but talks to me like I'm a wise-guy from the Bronx. I meet other bears with whom I behave as if we're pals from work, hanging out in the yard on the weekend. There's snappy banter and great visual gags, though I don't recall the details. Now that I consider it, I don't recall how I became a bear, or how I wandered from the bleak trashcan city to the snowmelt mountain wastes and back again. My head rattles like an old projector. How did I get here, to this trim cottage, in this perfect girl's bed, in a room lined with animal masks, my hungry tongue furred and my head blazing with distant stars?

THE SAILOR'S SONG

What I'd wished for was a black sea and a boat made of light, in a place where all rivers and rapids were reduced to pleasing alliteration and even steppingstones were nothing but a memorial hum. Instead, I found myself on a dead headland, with red waves lapping like cats at a milky Sun, while surf flossed rocky teeth and ships scuppered themselves ahead of any worse disaster. At the land's end, I lay down with the lamb and stripped it of its skin, folding its warm, wet fleece into a pillow for a companion who floated away before I even learned to pronounce her name. Sea became stars, became smoke, with nicotine stilling the nyctophobic judder, and I thought I saw a boat blinking like a beacon in the dark place where all explanations end. I wished for arms around me and palms pressed to the base of my spine. I wished for the song of the moorland spring where oceans are born. Then I tidied away time and tide and rolled them onto my tongue, where they tasted like something I was told never to put in my mouth.

SADNESS ISN'T ROCKET SCIENCE

Seaweed and tears: a new mother sits on a windswept dune, wrapping fine bones in her hair. She has piano hands and eyes like lullabies, lips like spaceships in bottles. Around her shoulders, a blanket woven from pawprints in snow is stitched with Jupiter's fifty-three named moons, from Adrastea to Thyone, with twenty-six blank lozenges for those still unbaptised. Her pulse is a song of embracing, from clavicle to carpals and to each distal phalange, and her love is *Gelidium longpipes* in harmony with the other 158 identified species of *Gelidiaceae*. And those tears, those tears are Earendel (OE: 'morning star'), 12.9 billion light years away. The fabric of space warps around galaxy cluster WHL0137-08, revealing sand and fingers with unprecedented clarity. Steadying breaths have commonly been tuned to 440 Hz since the early 1900s. Seaweeds, meanwhile, are known to produce umami flavour and are commonly used to make broths.

FINE TUNING THE SPIRIT GUIDE

Stars swill at the bottom of the bottle, glinting gold behind amber glass. Through cold measures of sky, a boy in blue cycles hard, his satchel crammed with the same news and weather he's been delivering since the invention of telescopes, cursive script, and pneumatic tyres. Today's top story is Pasiphaë/Pasiphae (pə'sɪfeɪ), the retrograde irregular satellite which Melotte first called Jupiter VIII. *What's in a name?* asks the tyke on the bike as the rolled-up paper splashes through air, but I was taught to care. *'She' is the Minotaur's mother,* as my grandmother often told me, slipper-shod in the forest, lading her apron with mushrooms that glowed like embryonic moons, though back when she was a girl nobody had even dreamed up a word for their taste. In the empty bottle, failed stars synthesise into gas giants, there are tyre tracks from my wrist to the eye of a four-hundred-year-old storm, and I have little but curling letters to pacify the unease of telescoping time.

THE BEST POSSIBLE TASTE

So, why do dogs with Heaven on top taste so good? Because, says the scientist bird, when it comes to the simplest points of their flesh, they are actually the sum of all existence. This is because fermentation/fur-mentation compounds their mammalian 'long sauce', popping one amino acid at a time. In a blindfold test, nine out of ten taste ancient leaves and mushrooms, high on coffee, with no-brainer meat hanging in a castle that only opens to visitors on rare Bank Holidays. Once inside, you must choose your cell carefully, then spade golden showers into the milk of humdrum kinkiness. Whip all flavours like a coarse cur. When you combine tastes containing these different kingdoms, they enhance one another, so even children transcend their soulless paper flavour. Any dog will do but it is essential to select your segments of Heaven with the same diligence with which you would choose, for example, a life partner, or just enough rope to hang yourself.

ENCOUNTERS WITH THE URBAN MYSTIC

It's a bad year and my clothes are older than my body. My coat was a soldier's and bears holes from the bullets that killed him. My cap belonged to a would-be shaman who skulked in the woods past my first school, living off roadkill and forage. He taught me my first spells, which mushrooms would kill you, and which mushrooms would stretch time so thin that you could look right through and wave to all those soldiers who'd marched down the road into lead and fire. Once I saw a man whose dry wounds matched the scorch-edged patterns of my coat but the wild man—for by then he had grown coarse fur like a scrawny bear—said not to pay it too much mind. Time, he told me, is little more than unlikely coincidence. Though it was another bad year, his words somehow made it less so. When his horns began to show, he gave me his cap.

THE WRONG PARTY

It's 1985, and the girl on every tabloid cover raises the perfect word as if it was a glass of Romanée Conti '45, aged to carmine and dancing in raspberry, rose petal, and spice. Though a native of Stratford-le-Bow, she terms it a *bon mot*, with a faultless Burgundian accent, whereas in my head it's always rhymed with Bon Scott, with its straining ground-glass bellow, oozing whisky, smoke, and fuck-right-off. So, I miss the *denouement* of her mannered tale, which she watches sail up to the crystal ceiling then fall like blossom or scattered light. She smiles on the surface of her *amor vincit omnia* eyes, and I try to respond in kind, but there's Malcolm Young grinding out a filthy riff full of sweat and innuendo, loose lips sink ships, and somewhere a clock strikes midnight.

SOUR

PAUL HETHERINGTON

*'I suppose any note, no matter how sour, sounds
like a song if you hold onto it long enough'*
—DeWitt Bodeen

CLIMBING

Teetering on the high flexing branch of the orchard's largest apple tree, you say 'It's sour as Christmas', and throw the bitten fruit. It bounces in grass and is inspected by a hen. You try another, saying 'This one's better', handing it to me and laughing as I nearly gag. A man comes running, waving us away. Years later you recollect how, having ducked under the wire fence, we kissed, with that bruised tartness swimming in our mouths.

CHERRIES

She's wrapped in her own arms, collecting ruminations within her body—as if it's a thought hoard, remembering *Beowulf's* eloquence. 'Wordhord onleac,' she murmurs, as if enjoining another to speak. Yet his sentences run like rain. Months of downpour and he won't apologise; he continually tries to sting her with words. Their divorce waits; new obligations encroach. Again, she looks inward, as if chewing thought, at a modest childhood next to an orchard. She recollects the tang of early cherries, and their blush unlocking sweetness. Like herself, she thinks—so long ago, before fomenting words.

PORTRAITS

'What should we do?' she asks. 'Where are we walking?' It's as if she speaks to the asphalt road, which returns his footsteps. There are no answers in her hands either; and no way to persuasively say 'love' again, despite their thirteen aching years. Mouthing the word leaves a sour taste. 'You?' he questions. His figure turns as sand gusts into her eyes. 'I'm not who you know,' she says, sensing the square buildings behind them and a broken fence. Later, she stands in her body as in a hall, and sees herself frowning in a dressing room mirror. He says, 'Don't forget the heritage I gifted you.' Centuries of portraits shine with darkening varnish.

GULL

Waves roll through consciousness, and a gull hovers on the gale as if stillness is a form of intent. It might be an emissary that words fail to address. A sour taste of wind, and the gull shifts higher, as if on Tetris blocks of air. Its spread wings flame but nothing melts, and thought is hoisted, until I see my father lifted to the unquantifiable sky on complex forms of speech, elevating his opaque care. Although no angel, he might be alive and circling on dark wings—an aged cherub once painted by Raphael. Gull-like, solitary, he searches for clearer air.

GREEN MAN

Naked at the edge of the track, this might be the Green Man returning. His skin is blotched with brown and red, as if bark has been torn from his body; he gibbers and shakes uncontrollably; he doesn't acknowledge the usual courtesies. People step away as he passes, though he doesn't attend to them; a train hisses leaving the station, and he jumps on, holding a railing and ducking inside the last carriage. Two passers-by shake their heads; the air fumes with diesel; he's a figment of lives we've left behind. The air he occupied gathers the scent of sour wild plants.

TIDES

You've known the tides washing over you for many seasons. You've swum across bays, heaving through the wintry ocean until your lungs were raw; you've hidden in stunted coastal scrub and smelt the sand's familiar sourness. All the time you've imagined yourself in other places, and still you wander in them, seeing old wrecks in a ship's graveyard, traipsing through mud in border country, detecting dropped metal in grassy fields. Or you're in the wild, hacking at roots and killing feral animals, with the seasons on top of you like long waves— scrutinising landmarks, patterns of sky and the unwieldy stars, sniffing sourgrass, building cairns, hunkering down.

MADRID

They were on the top floor of a Madrid hotel. She spent hours each day in the spa, reading *Clarissa*, drinking peppermint tea. He walked up and down, saying 'I need exercise'. At an illegal bar they got smashed on sour passionfruit margaritas. She said how much she was enjoying isolation—like a bubbly form of living in the past. He asked for whisky, talking about bad decisions—as if reiterating them might make a difference. 'American Pie' began and the bartender sang along. They drank Cointreau on ice and ruminated on the articulacy of eighteenth- and nineteenth-century writers, debating the broken structure of *Wuthering Heights*. In their hotel room she ran the bath, saying, 'Old literature really crowds the mouth'. He looked toward the heart of the city. 'Tomorrow,' he said. 'Let's plan for tomorrow.'

SHIFTING

The orchestra's sour note sat among Mozart's harmonies like an olive in a sweet apple pie. He shifted uncomfortably, hearing it again in the repetition of the theme. At interval they drank gin martinis and she reminded him of the green buoy they'd seen bouncing in a wide ocean's almost cerulean blue. 'Did you hear it?' she asked. They had swum out that day, rounding the buoy, handling each other eagerly in the surf, afterwards dozing on white sand. 'I'm in love,' she said, with her eyes closed, 'but not with you.'

APPASSIONATA

The famous pianist is going for all she's worth in the *Appassionata's allegro ma non troppo*, as if sound is an eloquent form of water or a machine for sucking in time. In the front stalls sits a woman he met three years ago, after a performance of Mozart's thirty-ninth symphony, when he talked about the sour eloquence of the opening movement and she talked about her dog—like some preposterous scene from Chekhov. The pianist stands to rapturous applause and he realises he's missed his favourite moment when the music gathers thought's darkness, along with the inveigling knowledge that deafness is surely permanent; knowing the clangorous protest of these chords solves nothing.

WHISKY SOUR

You read *Jerry Thomas' Bartenders Guide*, a modern reprint, and say the 'dry shake' must be performed—bourbon, lemon juice, sugar, egg white. Drapings of yellow light suggest luminous notions as you proffer a glass with frothed liquid. Outside your window the ocean rolls, suggesting this must pass. We loved each other when we were twenty, hiking through Cumbria to Castlerigg and standing within its ancient circle, drinking Whisky Sours. We tasted air in the mouth of winter as sky poured from above. The valley we entered was called a *cwm*, and *blaen* was where old gales raged. You circled my body with your arms and our restless language rejected comfort. Now we almost feel at home. You say, 'Not enough lovemaking and too many arguments', adding extra lemon to your glass.

CALAMANSI

The calamansi's a ruined kumquat, sour orange or corrupted lime. You dismiss the comparisons, making a *Sinigang sa kalamansi*, spooning it reverentially—food embedded in old traditions, flavours shadowed under the lintels of unwritten history, notions swelling and falling like bubbles. You sip and speak of the forty-eight years Americans colonised the Philippines, and of the Spanish before them. You say, 'Culture survives in bloody persistence', commenting on centuries of revolt and slaughter. Not knowing the history, I listen to names such as Gabriela Silang and Apolinario de la Cruz. The broth's tartness tastes like memory as you speak of the archipelago's profusion of languages; of rising seas that threaten the islands; of the sour taste of times like these.

LEMON

Squeezing lemon juice onto sugary pancakes, we dress our palates. You see a misty summer sun and smell the drift of citrus on your palm, speaking of your married life in Spain—'I remember that country like an acrid longing'. At night you turn the fruit as a moon rises through leaves; as a possum rasps. We make gin and tonics; we squeeze juice on tumbles of seafood and rice. You open a book of Flemish still lifes to show Jacob van Es's curling lemon peel: 'He used the motif over and over.' You talk of groves in Andalusia, and of Venetian limoncello. Sweet and tart marry in our mouths.

YOGHURT

You make it by hand, stirring gently until the starter vanishes, placing the bowl under a doona. Its sweet-sour simplicity reminds you of India where a bird watched from the windowsill as you flavoured yoghurt with mustard and cinnamon, following an ancient Mughal recipe. At the Qutb Shahi Tombs you considered the sultans who were supporters of learning and the Persian language—one a fine poet who founded Hyderabad. There you ate yoghurt with onions, chillis, cilantro and ginger and might have been thrown across centuries. Words teemed in your mouth that were never your own.

SEAWEEDS

You said, 'Seaweeds are commonly used in broths, and even in Korean porridge.' At Bonjuk in Seoul there were many choices of porridge: beef and Korean ginseng, hot abalone, clam rice with dried radish, or red crabmeat. Sweet pumpkin, too, and mung bean. You took me there as a way of saying, 'Breakfast has never been like this.' We walked toward a famous temple, past a stream long buried under a motorway. Your knowledge stretched beneath mine, flowing and chastening. Sweet, sour, bitter, salty—the savour of your words. I imagined your body wrapped in delicate seaweed as we swam through the mysteries of language; tasting its notions, finding its forms. You said 'Sour is best—and the salty piquancy of caress.'

SWEETNESS

'Love', you said, as if it were a sure path to sweetness; as if we could live within its boundaries like a house. We tried for a few months, sharing effervescing wine, but words crossed over to suggest a sourer life; an unkempt, arbitrary wantonness of speech; a sense of language refusing to conform. 'Love,' we repeated, like an unnerved charm. Yet acid words caroused in our mouths—suggestions of sharp flavours we had yet to try. And kisses, too, were acrid; your lovely lips were tart. 'Love', we said in intimate, sweet tones, tasting the word like spoiled, cheap champagne.

STARTING TO SWIM

The world's a front garden where unguarded bicycles lounge; and a back garden where carrots poke crookedly at air; and an old house with a sour smell, as if the nineteenth century turned to vinegar on its walls. Schoolchildren dawdle on the hill climbing toward primary school; its perimeter roads are shaded by peppermints—*agonis flexuosa*, as a teacher has said—and red flowering gums. The corridors smell of stale milk and tart injunctions; the girls are segregated on the top oval where handstands and skipping games precede the ringing of the school bell, and boys kick footballs on the bottom oval. I fly over the rectangular buildings, carried by shouts and laughter; birds veer as I flap like an awkward swan; the headmaster emerges from his office with Brylcreemed hair as grey as a slick tarmac. Landing, I swear at an older boy on a bike and he shakes his head, showing me a gap-toothed mouth. Abrupt rain gathers my legs until, floating down gutters, I hear my mother's voice shaping a strangled rendition of my name. The birds know me, ducking in and out of the downpour. I'm not far from the river now and, struggling against the current, I start to swim.

FRAGMENTS

2176, an anniversary. Daily feeds are flushed with history. We hear stories of unaugmented people, early computers and paper maps in fuming cars. Meanwhile the saccharine bulletins continue, and news of yet another war—they've recently raised the volume.

We worry micro-messages pollute the language, while maps are being re-drawn every year. My parents say they've heard it all before, but the colony on Mars wants new technicians.

I tell my girlfriend nothing's private, but she remarks, 'just stay as sour as you are'. In the meantime, I've joined a reading group rehabilitating history's black hole—old 'websites' no-one's read for years; bits of twentieth-century paper; slim, neglected volumes.

It's ludicrous how we care for poets' language. Though many channels carry thought elsewhere, their words insist on speaking out. My girlfriend says we need a deeper life. These broken fragments may yet dig us free.

BLEEDING HEART

i. Frangipani

It must be 2016 because a frangipani is growing next to the bedside table and a tropical vine is twining across the eaves. The snowy calyx and dangling crimson cause you to exclaim 'bleeding heart', as we tuck ourselves under intersecting waterfalls. You're dressed in blooms of the Madagascar Jasmine; I'm holding the pebbled rind of a Seville orange, considering the history of marmalade. Our histories are the words of Odin's loquacious ravens, or the speaking bird from the Sicilian tale, or a lost tale by Chrétian de Troyes. And your language is one I'm trying to learn; you say it has roots in archaic culture when poetry was sung among sacred places, and it's lovely as water on an ancient causeway. You say the Maya worshipped the frangipani; that this is a deity you can admire.

ii. Philodendron

It must be 2017, because the bleeding-heart vine has colonised the laundry, its roots exploring the bathtub and foliage grasping at light. You're wearing the lance-like leaves of the philodendron, stitched with red wool, and I'm making tea from woodsorrel sourgrass. The air conditioner's permanently set to high and, though it's autumn, you sleep with a cotton sheet barely wrapping your legs. Three species of panicum are edging the bed, there are blue morpho butterflies eyeing the windowsill, a poison dart frog climbs from the sink. 'I adore the postman,' you say, 'because he brings me champagne', as you pour a Blanc de Blanc into two large tumblers. We stand on the balcony as raindrops sting our shoulders; you press your glass to the exquisite curve of your belly, talking of the Olmec's reverence for the jaguar; the animal as a water god. 'Time immemorial,' you say, holding your arms and face to the rain.

iii. Waterlily

It must be 2018, because the bed is resting on a monstrous water lily—*Victoria amazonica*—and you're swimming toward it in one-piece bathers made from the leaves of canna lilies. Your pale legs frog-kick until you turn to loll in filtered sunshine, hearing the splashing of river dolphins. On another leaf, someone's reading poems from a forgotten culture whose language has a sibilance of moistened tongues. You found an expert in a university corridor and brought her home to teach you Greek. A green anaconda slides. You speak of the serpent as a pathway to visions; of losing skin and transformation. The bleeding-heart vine has become our canopy; the ancient poems fall like drizzle. 'Poems of ritual—of marriage and death.' You say it reflectively, as if peeling language from painful lips; as if breathing sharp fumes from an earthenware vessel.

iv. Papyrus

It must be 2019 because the canna lily has wilted and the river dolphins have vanished upstream. We divide the bleeding-heart vine into twenty pots and you plant them close to the *Cyperus papyrus*. You are chewing the pith of its youngest shoots, carrying blooms of the lotus and singing poems in the language of Sappho. I say it sounds pungent but you dismiss the 'bright crassness we've all got used to'. We might be in a reed boat holding fragments of ancient poetry and watching out for hippopotami as the Nile floods. The name Anactoria is like a struck chord; the presence of time is thick as humidity; we feel our bodies wet with longing. Back in our bedroom you suggest I swim 'through perspiration, kissing my lips', and we become like Hapi among inundation, coloured strangely and chorused by frogs.

SWEET

PAUL MUNDEN

I

'My enemies have sweet voices
their tones are soft and kind
when I hear my heart rejoices
and I do not seem to mind'
       —Pete Morgan

GINGERBREAD HOUSE

Whatever led you here, your memory has erased, like those doubling-back breadcrumbs eaten by birds.

The house is welcoming enough—too much so, perhaps—with its gingerbread walls pebble-dashed with hundreds and thousands, its Battenberg roof tiles, sugar-glass windows and the deeply panelled dark chocolate front door.

It's pretty as Christmas, but it's here you'll be fattened, in place of the goose.

And even though you maintain morale, there has only been one known escape, a fact you cheerfully ignore.

LOVE HEARTS

They appeal to your sweet tooth, in a pack of 21. Their 'pretty please' messages are a match for the fizz of sherbet on your tongue: a cute trail of emojis in pastel colours; a sentimental journey; a romance. KISS ME / DREAM BOY / LET'S DANCE / HUG ME / BE MINE / TRUST ME / LOVE ME / MARRY ME . . . What's not to like?

The sequence, though, is random. And some hearts seem less innocent: RU WET? / EAT ME / BLOW ME . . . not necessarily your style, but you can live with it.

The bigger shock is the pack that begins GROW UP!—and gets worse: YOU SUCK / I HATE YOU / DROP DEAD / BYE!

And yet you smile, popping them one by one into your mouth.

TOAD

The full range of temptation is wheeled to your table, the
trolley groaning under the weight of what should be
light as air. The problem is both variety and the size
of the portions; the irresistible also *too much*, more
challenge than treat.

THE STICKY TOFFEE PUDDING
SQUATS LIKE A THICK-SET SLOBBERING TOAD
ON THE PLATE. YOU'RE GETTING INDIGESTION JUST
STARING IT IN THE FACE, BUT ITS TREACLY
EXPRESSION BEATS YOU DOWN.

As you finish the final spoonful, the waitress comes to ask you
how it was. *Excellent, excellent,* you whisper, more like
a final gasping for breath before they wheel you out.

AMMO

The wine runs out. Also the beer. And *why is the rum always gone?* In desperation you shove *Pirates of the Caribbean* into the hard-to-find DVD slot of the TV. How long, you wonder, does it take to turn molasses into liquid gold? And will Johnny Depp even help?

You're drifting, but later—rummaging in the shed—you find the gun-belt of single-shot liqueurs. You're in mini-bar heaven. They're firing at your ship but you don't give a damn.

You wake upside down, around noon, not on a paradisiacal island beach but in a swivelling Habitat chair in the upper-floor living room of your student digs, your hair sticky with Tia Maria, and a hangover from hell.

Time to reload.

SWEET FA

There's surely a difference between *sweet nothings* and an army ration can of what looks, you joke, like Fanny Adams' remains. Google, disinterested, simply takes you to the English Football Association.

'After Spurs had taken the lead, James Ward-Prowse hit two free kicks so sweetly that the Saints went marching in.'

Hit . . . sweetly. . . A ball, yes, but not a woman, oh no. Then you're a sinner, good and proper. You don't, ever, *want to be in that number.*

A DAY IN THE LIFE

John Lennon counts the song in with 'sugar-plum-fairy, sugar-plum-fairy' ...

The eponymous ballerina tiptoes on stage in satin bodice and Disney skirt, layered with tulle. Hoffman's dark fairy-tale battle has been saccharined into dance. Everyone's enthralled by the crystalline sound of the celesta Tchaikovsky stumbled on in Paris, 1891, a perfect music box/toy box match.

She's Tinkerbell without the attitude, but somewhere inside her a firefly burns. And today is the day she finally calls it a day, traipsing off into the wings with fallen arches and a rant replete with dropped aitches and expletives.

She retreats into a haze of whatever narcotics are available, drifting through strawberry fields, marmalade skies and marshmallow pies.

She soaks in absinthe, moonshine, 100 proof, listening to B Bumble and the Stingers. 'Nutrocker', LOUD. But that's just a sugar rush, mere Tate & Lyle before Emerson Lake & Palmer: cocaine.

Snow-blind, she falls into the glass-fronted cabinet, severing her aorta.

CANDYMAN

His aftershave is sickly sweet, but you don't know that when you find him on the Sugar Dating site.

If this is what it takes to pay your way through university, so be it; you're nobody's fool. But his inclinations are a trifle odd. He offers you chocolate cigarettes, sometimes the white candy ones, with red tips to make you believe they're lit. Perhaps he'd been in the Prince Charles Cinema, Soho, when the uncut *Emmanuelle* was first shown.

He wants you to brush his teeth, to sugar wax his chest.

Stuff with Mars Bars is a favourite, not to your taste. Your sweet spot isn't really in his repertoire.

They say revenge is sweet. Your degree in hand, you marshal a posse of friends to truss your Sugar Daddy up and smother him in honey. The bees from his vandalised hive do the rest.

II

'To bend with apples the moss'd cottage-trees,
And fill all fruit with ripeness to the core;
To swell the gourd, and plump the hazel shells
With a sweet kernel'

—John Keats

TREES

The silver birch you planted in Pete's memory has a plaque at the base with your favourite line, the one about *sweet voices*. Sometimes you used to feel that poetry was the enemy, however silvered its song. The tree is tall and straight, commanding a view of both your small garden and Rowntree Park.

In my garden are two fruit trees, christening gifts for my daughters, who've left home. It's mainly windfall apples that I gather; I cook them, but they're sweet enough to need no sugar. The old black lab used to steal all the pears. This year, I plan to harvest them, taking the weight of each fruit in my hand, but they won't fall.

Next day, they've vanished.

CHOCOLATE

The aroma of roasting cocoa pervades the whole city. You can taste the very air. Sometimes there's a fine chocolate dusting, everywhere, a sepia tone turning eventually to pure theme park, with Chocolate Emporium, Chocolate Workshops and Chocolate Story Museum. The old factory buildings are now luxury apartments. Beside the railway tracks into the station, a billboard startles the tourists with *Welcome to York where the chocolate's chunky and the men are hunky!*—the story re-rated from PG to 18.

CHRISTMAS

After this shittiest of years, with the cost of living spiralling way way out of control, the pound in your pocket is almost worthless. Mary Poppins is on TV as usual, with her reliable spoonful of sugar to make the economic medicine go down, but feeding the birds seems too fanciful by far. For the first time in his life, the Governor of the Bank of England uses the term 'apocalyptic'. But there, as you twist your hand towards the toe of your Christmas stocking—the huge seaman's sock from your grandfather's days in the navy—past the obligatory mandarin, satsuma, tangerine or clementine, is an orange mesh bag of chocolate money that right now is so, so much better than what passes for the real thing. You peel away the disks of gold foil and place a coin in your mouth, letting its sweet currency dissolve into a pleasant craving for more.

SWEETNESS AND LIGHT

Your signature Lemon Posset calls for the smallest silver
    spoons, and the miniature schooners otherwise
    reserved for your homemade limoncello.

But how do I deal with this finesse—me with my big paws,
    more used to flicking salmon from the river, that
    Hughesian *river of light*?

THE LAND OF COCKAIGNE

Someone set up an Easter egg hunt and got carried away. The whole landscape is speckled with tiny eggs wrapped in silver and gold. They nestle in the crook of every candied branch of every candied tree. Meadows of sugared almonds and pear drops are a-hum with marzipan bees. There are rivers of lemonade, rivers of wine, lakes of milk and pools of honey; clouds of pink candyfloss, like a never-ending sunset. Bushfires, though rare, leave the whole territory reeking of burnt sugar.

Some accounts tell of naked honeybuns (nuns?) bathing in the streams, though it's hard to say how that could be verified. It seems gratuitous—or is that the point?

In the capital, Konfektburg, the cake-built houses are faintly reminiscent of a childhood ordeal, but I've never seen such barley sugar porticos, with fondant canopies, nor this maze of pastry-paved streets with their chocolate Wagon Wheeled cars.

The Konditor has decreed that nothing in this mouth-watering utopia need be paid for, and I finally get my bearings. I'm back in the school tuck shop, c.1968, any purchase billed to my parents' account.

Six kaleidoscopic years down the line, it's a different story, sugar—and coal—in short supply. The government introduces a three-day week. It's hardship of a sort—no icing for the Christmas cake, and no TV after 10 p.m. We do our homework by candlelight. One day somebody's desk catches fire.

I realise I've never bought a bag of sugar since, like some eighteenth-century Anti-Saccharist, its production still relying on slaves. When the plumber asks for two spoonfuls, I'm dumbstruck, as if facing the Easter Bunny.

A COTTAGE GARDEN

You climb the hill through a glade of sweet chestnuts, into the garden where you are gradually learning the plants by name, even though it wasn't you who planted them. It's the name and specific memory that counts, not their meaning; you're not Ophelia. The multi-coloured, fragrant Sweet Peas she chose to sow from scratch every year, twisting around a skeletal wigwam of canes; the sturdier Sweet William, filling out the borders, clumps of flowers clustered by butterflies and bees; and the Honeysuckle still hugging the warm stone wall above the terrace where she would sit with a glass of red wine.

LA DOLCE VITA

The dour, sun-creased Sicilian is stationed at the bar as ever, 7 a.m., as you breeze in on your way to the language school and place your usual order, having to insist on *no sugar.*

Every day the Sicilian scowls. Finally he speaks: *Life is bitter— coffee is sweet.* But you're quick and strong with your reply: *No, coffee is bitter—life is sweet.*

The Sicilian is silent, but from now, every day, he acknowledges you with a grudging smile.

III

'Goodnight sweet ladies, all ladies goodnight. . .
It's a lonely Saturday night'

—*Lou Reed*

MERINGUE

Such was the memory couched within the taste—even the word itself—that every time he saw *meringue* on the menu, he would pause, his poem with her imaginary words once more on his lips, as

> *her spoon touched his, dipping into the creamed meringue … The bottle empty, they sat in silence, wondering how long the waiter might take to bring them the bill, if they should split it, or if some initiative beyond their known competence night be required*

… his ability to decide on a course of action—even this iteration of choosing dessert—having stalled yet again.

NOTES TOWARDS A SONG

Ain't She ——— , ———Creature , ———Thing , ——— ———Baby ,
——— Lady , ——— Caroline , ——— Child o' Mine ,
———Cherry Wine , ——— About Me , My ——— Lord ,
———Sixteen , ——— Emotion , ——— Talkin' Woman ,
——— Talking Guy , ——— Gene Vincent , Swing Low
———Chariot , ——— Home Alabama , ——— Virginia ,
——— Surrender , ——— Jane , How ——— It Is (to be
loved by you) , ——— Seasons , Sail Away ——— Sister ,
———Miracle , ———Melody , ———Dreams (Are Made
of This) , ——— Thames flow softly, till I end . . .

YESTERDAY

You woke with the immaculate tune, no words. You foraged
   for something that would fit; it was time for breakfast,
   lodging in your girlfriend's house: *scrambled eggs*?

The perfect bittersweet anthem needed work. And all the
   while your young love drifted away; your troubles there
   to stay.

In her children's party book of 1988, scrambled eggs are off
   the menu. But there's a beehive cake, and edible bees
   with gelatine wings.

HONEY PIE

Or is she *honeybun*, *honeybunch*, or any number of American pseudonyms for *my darling*, tripping off the tongue? It's a roll call of all those rock chicks you slept with, back in the day when you were their *boy lollipop*, making their hearts *go giddy-up*, before they shrugged and set out for Sugar Mountain, leaving you behind.

Sometimes, as the years go by, you write songs of regret. Sometimes you just gorge yourself on fortune cookies, looking for a sign—that your one true sweetheart will return.

They say honey 'will last, uncorrupted, for a thousand years. People have eaten honey from the tombs of the pharaohs. They say it is good as gold.'

WHERE THE LOST THINGS GO

Mary Poppins returns, with songs re-born after fifty-four
years, like poppies in the freshly-ploughed twelve-acre
field above my garden.

Inside, when I sieve flour, particles of memory are similarly
refined. I stir, make a wish, as I did in my mother's
kitchen, eating the uncooked cake mix off a plastic
spatula straight from the bowl.

My daughters grew up with a giant, screen-printed strawberry
on the dining room wall. It still hangs there, presiding
over fewer parties, fewer meals.

Mary, how well you grasp that the lost dish and spoon are
just collateral to the greater absence—*her touch | And
loving gaze*. But also—and *maybe* is as strongly as
you'll put it—that those we miss are still within us.

SWEET BIRD OF YOUTH

They all had the requisite blue eyes, Newman, McQueen . . .
could play King Lear one night, comedy the next.

As Junior Bonner, McQueen comes home for a final rodeo,
not so much for fame or renown as reconciliation with
his family, only to find his brother bulldozing their old
house for a tacky new development. His father, Ace,
dreams of heading to Australia, mining for gold.

Somehow JR pulls it off. Not so Chance Wayne, actor turned
gigolo, returning to St Cloud, the attributes of his
youth long gone. His one-time sweetheart, Heavenly,
is no longer a match for her name, and the town-folk
are vindictive. A gruesome fate is in store for Chance,
and yet for Newman the ending is—how shall we say—
fudged; it's to give us all hope.

HOMEWARD BOUND

After the meeting, we rush to board the train, and order drinks.
Our conversation gradually slows. Tired, you close your
eyes. As you fall asleep, your head tilts gently sideways
until it rests on my shoulder. I try not to move, to hold
the moment for the remaining hour, seven minutes and
fifteen seconds it takes for the train to reach York, and
for the years beyond, thinking only *sweet dreams*.

NOTES

A Day in the Life: The Sugar Plum Fairy is a character in E.T.A. Hoffman's tale, 'The Nutcracker and the Mouse King', adapted by Alexandre Dumas and turned into a ballet, *The Nutcracker*, by Tchaikovsky in 1892. 'Nutrocker' by B. Bumble and the Stingers, later covered by Emerson, Lake & Palmer, was potentially subject to a BBC ban on parodies of classical music, but ultimately deemed inoffensive.

Candyman: The featured 'revenge' is taken from the 1992 film, *Candyman*, directed by Bernard Rose.

Sweetness and Light: The closing phrase is from Ted Hughes' poem, 'That Morning', from *River* (Faber & Faber, 1983).

The Land of Cockaigne: 'Le Fabliau de Cocagne' (The Land of Plenty) is a 13th-century French poem, though 'Cucania' was mentioned in the earlier *Carmina Burana*. A 14th-century English poem picks up the baton, and so it continues. London 'Cockney' may even be related. In *The Nutcracker*, the Land (of Sweets) is under the temporary rule of the Sugar Plum Fairy.

Meringue: The poem quoted, also titled 'Meringue', was published in *Chromatic* (UWA Publishing, 2017).

Yesterday: Jane Asher was Paul McCartney's girlfriend when the song was written. Her book, *Jane Asher's Children's Parties*, was published by Michael Joseph in 1988.

Honey Pie: McCartney's song of the same name was included on the Beatles' so-called *White Album* (1968). The closing quotation is from *Ever After* (Picador, 1992) by Graham Swift.

Sweet Bird of Youth: The title refers to a 1959 play by Tennessee Williams. It was made into a film with Paul Newman, in 1962, with a radically changed ending. *Junior Bonner* (1972), starring Steve McQueen, was directed by Sam Peckinpah.

BITTER

JEN WEBB

'She gorged on bitterness without a name'
—Christina Rossetti

'I give you bitter pills in sugar coating. The pills are
harmless: the poison is in the sugar'
—Stanislaw Lec

'in chambering and wantonness and in deafness and
death and bitter and blind bawling against the honey'
—Samuel Beckett

GORGING ON BITTERNESS

The groceries failed to arrive. Our dinner was diverted to a different street. And here we are at table, fork and knife in hand, and empty plates. Last year's frustrations have given way to mild acceptance, now the planet has spun on its heel and sniffed at us, coldly. I fight my way past squabbling galahs to the garden bed, where remnants of last season's greens are hanging on. Arugula; dandelion; all the bitter herbs. I bring them in a basket, and we dip them in vinegar and oil as though for a feast.

WITHOUT A NAME

They purr like distant traffic, dream the crunching of bones, and I sit with them under the half empty moon, imagining the blood of mine enemies. The world turns; the cats stretch, their claws extended, and I stretch too. How little gravity means on a night like this. How long the tendrils of burnt hope. Tonight we will stand under the banksia tree, studying its remnant candles. Your broken son will join us, and all the dead you carry with you, airmen still fighting the controls all the way down, soldiers not yet game to lift their heads above the wall.

EXECUTING THE WILL

The hall is full of words. We talk of illness and death; of sweetness; the care of the corpse. It's not a bitter truth, as such, but it is nonetheless true. Graves. Flowers on graves. *In the midst of life we are in death,* the priest intoned, and you replied *and vice versa,* shocking the soldiers who stand to attention in every century. Your timing is off, my dear. You lift a corner of the darkness and find the light someone else swept there. I draw my finger through the light, casting shadow, tracing a name in chiaroscuro.

QUESTION TIME

The speaker is approaching the borders of silence: I recognise the stutter in his rhythm; he is beginning to doubt the power of words. I could sweeten his day if I intervened—if I called for questions, scraped a Dorothy Dixer off the floor of my mind. If, if. If passion lived up to promise, if tradesmen ceased to ring our bell, if the trees shook loose their own limbs. *If wishes were horses*, says my grandmother out of the distant past. Dear speaker, the night is settling in. Put up your sword. Call it a day.

HELPS THE MEDICINE GO DOWN

He brought me grapefruit on a Wedgwood plate, a serrated spoon set at an angle on its right. Eat, he said; bitter food is good for you; and when my tongue shrank back from the taste, he sprinkled salt across the cut face of the fruit, and fed me a segment, and I ate it, listening to Saariaho's *Folia*, finding at last a taste for the texture of bass.

RETRENCHED

I select black for the plumb-bob line I'll never use, resist the whites and reds in the paint aisle, load bags of mulch onto the aching trolley. I should buy mouse traps, ant poison, rakes. Should load up on paint stripper and mattocks. I wheel past the café, eyeing up the honey cakes that are on display. Pick up and discard a craft knife; consider queueing at the sausage sizzle to exchange five bucks for a sense of community. No one sees me pass. I queue at the tills then drift away, unobserved. Leave the trolley in the car park; wonder if I can find my way back home.

TESTING THE GUSTATORY CORTEX

Today's word is 'combing'. You say it slowly, enunciating. Taste in its letters the citrus peel, the spinach, the spice. You've not eaten for months, not proper food, but every day you place a word on your tongue and savour the bitter C, buttery M, the sharp serifs of the G. All the papillae on your tongue shiver— some for pleasure, some for pain, as your nerves measure the senses, write their reports. Spit out the letters, lick your fingers clean. Tomorrow's word will be 'symphony', and its taste will remind you of delight.

✳

BEYOND STEENBRAS

You badly wanted to go to the shops with your friends but no it's a Sunday which is to say Familyday so you're piled into the car with your sisters for the long drive down through the suburbs to the high coast road where your parents teach you to see what they see, stopping the car, saying *Look! We're at the edge of the world!*

Beyond the car, beyond the waters and the waves, the edge. There is nothing but deep ocean, and three slow ships making their way over and down to what you can't see from here— Australia; the South Pole; outer space. It's lonely. You feel lonely in this world that is too broad and too empty, knowing you have nothing to say that it cares to hear. The car moves on, then stops again beside the lookout at the top of the pass, and mum passes back fruit and sandwiches, and soon the baboons are there too, banging on the windows, all teeth and arse and loud demands. Some Sunday. Some goddamn day.

ON FORGETTING

Necessary to keep one's hair washed and brushed, clothes groomed, let no one with their clipboards make notes about this disturbance or that mistake. Mudlarks in the garden, pigeons saying *whooo*, lizards lying doggo in the sun.

I do the laundry on weekends and clean the house from up to down; wash myself daily and dress in front of the full-length mirror, seeing who I was in healthier years. *Mum?* I call out in the deep night. *Are you there?* The theme tune of her life, and mine.

❋

BITTER PILLS

When the contractor called we stared at the number that stared back at us from the face of the phone, but we didn't pick up. When he took to banging on the front door and then the back we took to lying under the bed, breathing sotto voce, holding hands for courage. Your fear is all over my skin and when night hides us I stand under the shower, scrubbing. Later, in the small hours, we lie awake, holding hands for courage, and tell each other tales of a future when all obligations have faded, when men with clipboards and phones have forgotten we exist. We no longer check the mail. We've deleted the email apps. Silence swells about us, like snow, like stone.

SUGAR COATING

We clear the garden according to the rules, spreading green matter then cardboard then green matter then leaves. We clear the fridge and shake out radishes and rose petals for heart's blood, scatter fenugreek and cumin for courage, sugar cane for structural integrity. When the inspectors arrive they walk slowly back and forth across the site, hands clasped behind their backs. Sometimes they murmur into a throat mic, sometime scoop up a sample. We stand with our backs to the wall, straight-spined as soldiers but with fingers hooked together for consolation. If they acknowledge the story we are trying to tell. If they tick the 'yes' boxes on their forms. If they see the beauty of the worm beneath the skin.

POISON IN THE SUGAR

This is the day they wake from dreams of drowning for no good reason. Someone brings tea they cannot drink, chocolate made of mud. Someone brings a map of the fire exits and instructions about where to meet should the disaster occur. He looks out the window, past her gesticulating hand. Traffic is building: a red bus goes by, then a purple bus, then another red, each of them juddering, wheezing, old workers who are undervalued, underpaid. Someone shakes her by the shoulder, someone is holding the door for them, are they expected to step through? *Do I have slippers?* she says, *A robe?* He says, *Is there time to find my way?*

I WAS TOLD I'M A SUPER TASTER

Oddly enough, she says, *I quite like Brussels sprouts*, and from across the room he replies, *I just don't like them. I tried. I wanted to like them, I didn't.*

What does geography taste like? *Maybe like coffee, or oranges, bitter but sweet.* Dark chocolate peppered with glass, Brussels served with soda.

Brussel sprouts are scrumptious and better than cake. So what does cake taste like? *At first it'd be horrid then the sweetness would explode in your mouth, suddenly, delicious. Like Brussel sprouts, they are delectable, I would eat a whole bowl for lunch.*

The magpie pecks at the cashews she's tossed across the verandah, looks at her with side eye, then scoops up the rest and heads back to the nest where Magpie 2 is cooking their eggs.

What do magpies taste like? *Fucking disgusting and bitter and terrible and if you disagree you need to start treating yourself better.* Bitter taste is linked to hostile thoughts, says the scholar.

Nutmeg in the keyboard, grapefruit in the bath. *Bitter taste in my mouth. Is it the alcohol that's inside my system or is it the other way around?*

✳

AT THE SWISS CLINIC

She is no longer young, as the crone in the mirror reminds
her, pointing out that only the young are beautiful, but she
shrugs that off—she's *been* young!—and every message in a
bottle is only an overdue bill, and now she's living off what
she's gained, knowing when to apply the *this'll do, mate* that
gets her past many an awkward scene. And after all, how old
is too old? Axiologists wrangle the algorithms then settle on a
number that makes sense. She shrugs it off, pushes her front
door to. She has broken all her mirrors and, not watching, she
slides into a deep bath, and sighs.

IN CHAMBERING AND WANTONNESS

Stone scrapes on stone. Cast a watchful eye at the snow clouds that brood along the mountains that have clearly drawn closer overnight. Plants communicate possibilities; local rabbits glance up, wisdom in their gaze and we strip off our clothes beneath the sky, dance and fuck for fertility then collect the necessary herbs I will dry beside the kitchen stove, and store for later need. The lawn is turning up its toes, thistles and stickyweed colonising the garden, your wife has run away with the moon, and I hug my blanket, lock the windows and the doors, take my comforts where I can. On dark nights I move around the suburb, murmuring remedies to those who seem to be in need.

IN DEAFNESS AND IN DEATH

Your mother's ghost waits at the edges of your life, her outline sketched by clairvoyants, her heart beating in some new arrangement of Bach's famous fugue. You explain this to your therapist, and he terms it a demanding nonsense, and slices it into sense.

Light a smudge stick; your mother synthwaves into view, accompanied by the bittersweet scent of joy, and she's you as you will be when your mouth stiffens, eyelids fall. You see the planes of her younger self in the mirror where you stand, candle in one hand, broomstick in the other. You whimper, softly, but one look from her and that nonsense stops.

＊

BITTER AND BLIND

He has gone into hiding, though when he called, he called it hibernation, and best, he said, I get on with my own life, at least for now.

I get on. Pacing the back garden, sending hate-mail to the pope.

There's a midnight drunk at the back door, squinting into the security lights; a rabbit peering in through the glass. The man across the way introduces me to mild flirtation, and I roll its taste across my tongue.

I am getting on, learning how to read the seasons, learning again how to see the world through one clear eye.

BAWLING AGAINST THE HONEY

It's not only that he raises a perfect eyebrow in his sub-evidentiary sneer but that as we both know he categorises us and all we love as—subfusc?—is that the word? Anyway I felt condescended to and as such retracted my mild sexual curiosity. *Correlation*, he observes, *is not causation*, but he knows we already know and we tip our glasses his way, ironically, and gulp don't sip the wine. Subfusc I now recall is not the right word; substandard is what I was reaching for. You haul me away though I'm spoiling for more wine and for a fight, and now we're home, you cooking the rice and me staring glumly into the almost empty fridge.

FIRE SEASON

What we're thinking as we stare into the sun is only *well, who knows?* Sparks clog our eyes, pollen clogs our throats, and we are treading water in an oubliette. The radioman says don't go out, no one can breathe this air. We're outside already though, catching handsful of waste in the city storm. Looks like snow, you say, but it tastes like toxins, bitter and cold. The radioman says there's lead; the radioman says watch out for sulphur. Google says: The page you are trying to view doesn't exist. We take shelter under what's left of the roof and spend the day breathing, drawing tally marks on the wall. Heights are wuthering; light is shuddering; we've forgotten how to touch each other, or ourselves.

MINJERRIBAH

It takes an hour through flukey water—now ankle high, now grabbing at my waist—before I reach the sandbar where waves are spuming, their hands full of sand, and gulls are reaping the bitter fish. Your child is on the beach, digging a redoubt; my child rests on his elbow, staring at the sun. I starfish in the water, face down, till the sea rolls me to and fro like a whale, logging. This is where we came in, blown on the tide, committing to a future that starts with cautious flipper on sand, imagining what it's like to live on land.

AN ANTHROPOLOGIST AT LARGE

Listing the things they eat; analysing their tastes. It's slabs of seaweed drawn cold from the shore and sliced; code it umami. It's fine clay textured with tiny stones and washed down with black water from the well that long ago was sealed. Code it sour. Spoonsful of mustard for strong bones, chewed in the company of cranberries. That's bitter, like dry bread for bad children, like cardamon you bite by mistake. They eat what I would not eat, and their skin glows, so at night when they dance there is no need for lamps. Their feet describe slow circles, an arm about a lover's waist. I sketch the scene, think I might understand if I watch long enough, if I can learn to see.

NOTES

Helps the Medicine Go Down: According to a number of studies into taste, bass sounds are closely affiliated with bitter tasting foods. See Crisinel, Anne-Sylvie and Charles Spence 2009 'Implicit Association between Basic Tastes and Pitch', *Neuroscience Letters* 464, 39–42. Kaija Saariaho's *Folia* (1995), referenced in this poem, is written for double bass with live electronics; in an interview Saariaho explains that her compositional practice depends on: 'Different senses, shades of colour, or textures and tones of light, even fragrances and sounds blend in my mind' (cited Moisala, Pirkko 2009 *Kaija Saariaho,* Urbana, IL: University of Illinois Press, 55).

Retrenched: Studies show a correlation between colours and tastes, one that is consistent across cultures. Black is associated with bitter, white with salt, yellow with sour, and pink or red with sweet. See Spence, Charles et al. 2015 'On Tasty Colours and Colourful Tastes? Assessing, Explaining, and Utilizing Crossmodal Correspondences Between Colours and Basic Tastes', *Flavour* 4:23.

I was told I'm a super taster: This is redacted from a sequence of responses to a dietician's research into the taste of bitter foods. The phrases in italics are rendered as they were in the original, hence 'Brussel' rather than the more correct 'Brussels' in some phrases.

✵ ◎ ✳ ✿ ✺

INDIVIDUAL
POETS' STATEMENTS

CASSANDRA ATHERTON

Once known as 'white gold', salt was, historically, a 'precious commodity that played an important part in the development of the ancient world' (Elias 2020, 19). Indeed, the etymology of the word 'salary' demonstrates that wages were paid in salt. Today, salt is perhaps best known as a popular table condiment—a flavour enhancer, and also a preservative. We need salt to survive, and yet over-consumption of salt can be deadly. Salt is also thought to ward off evil or black magic, and rings of salt or salt circles are believed to protect those who stand inside them.

In his introduction to his book *Salt: A World History*, Mark Kurlansky notes the way salt captured the imaginations of writers and philosophers: 'Homer calls it a divine substance [and] Plato describes it as especially dear to the Gods' (2002, 3). Kurlansky also unearths Welsh psychologist Ernest Jones's obsession with salt and its connection to sex in Jones's essay 'The Symbolic Significance of Salt in Folklore and Superstition', highlighting '[the] fact that the customs and beliefs relating to salt are exactly parallel to those relating to sexual secretions and excretions' and 'the complex and far-reading way in which the salt-idea is interwoven with matters of sex, particularly with potency and fertilization' (1921, 51).

This is no doubt linked to the definition, dating back to 1866, of 'salty' as piquant or racy, applied to humour relating to sex. In another common slang definition, perhaps dating back to the 1580s, salty has come to mean being angry, annoyed or upset at something unimportant. The internet has many sites dedicated to publishing people's discussions of why they are salty.

In cooking, Samin Nosrat argues that salt is not only salty but it works to transform other flavours:

> salt has a greater impact on flavour than any other ingredient... Salt's relationship to flavour is multidimensional: it has its own particular taste and it enhances the flavour of other ingredients. Used properly, salt minimises bitterness, balances out sweetness, and enhances aromas, heightening our experience of eating. (2017, n.p.)

With the rise in television cooking shows over the last few decades, salt is back on the table, quite literally, as celebrity chefs are often shown adding large pinches of salt to enhance their food. There is even a Turkish chef, Nusret Gokce, dubbed 'Salt Bae', who has a meme based on the signature style he has of seasoning his meat.

Finally, idioms such as 'worth one's salt', 'salt of the earth', 'take it with a grain of salt' and 'pour salt on the wound' show the prevalence of salt in the use of metaphors and its importance in language.

A note on the format: I have always been haunted (or perhaps even taunted) by choice. At school, I felt anxious when I read Robert Frost's 'The Road Not Taken' with its pivotal fork in the road. A seemingly inconsequential decision can potentially profoundly affect future experience. For this reason, my collection of prose poems has a sliding doors structure—named after the 1998 film of the same title, but explored earlier by J.B. Priestly in *Dangerous Corner* (1932) and Krzysztof Kieślowski in *Blind Chance* (1987). Most recently, it has been introduced to a new generation in *Look Both Ways* (2022) on Netflix. The sliding doors structure is similar to the idea of a parallel universe or the reverberations discussed in the butterfly effect, and is also connected to other creative time-bending in films such as *Groundhog Day* (1993), *It's A Wonderful Life* (1946), and the TV series *Russian Doll* (2019).

In my sequence of paired prose poems, the first work sets up a traumatic moment that is a catalyst for the protagonist exploring her experience across two different lives. To help the reader differentiate, the first prose poem in each pair is written in the second person, 'you', followed by a prose poem that uses the third person, 'he'. In this way, prose poems with the same title are explored from two different angles.

Works Cited

Elias, Miguel, Marta Laranjo, Ana Cristina Agulheiro-Santos and Maria Eduarda Potes 2020 'The Role of Salt on Food and Human Health', in *Salt in the Earth*, edited by Mualla Cengiz and Savas Karabulut, London: Intertech Open

Jones, Ernest 1921 'The Symbolic Significance of Salt in Folklore and Superstition', in *Essays in Applied Psycho-analysis*, London: The Hogarth Press Ltd and The Institute of Psycho-Analysis

Kurlansky, Mark 2002 *Salt: A World History*, London: Jonathan Cape

Nosrat, Samin 2017 *Salt, Fat, Acid, Heat: Mastering the Elements of Good Cooking*, Edinburgh: Canongate Books

OZ HARDWICK

In 1908, the Japanese chemist Kikune Ikeda proposed the existence of a distinct basic taste, for which he coined the name *umami* (うま味). Following this, it was nearly eight decades before the term was recognised and adopted by the scientific community at the first Umami International Symposium, held in Hawaii in October 1985.[1]

I am not a scientist but I am an omnivorous nerd, so a couple of things fascinated me about this information. First amongst these was the fact that it took around, say, 200,000 years of tottering around on two legs, stuffing all and sundry into our mouths to check out what worked and what didn't, to one day have someone suggest that, *maybe, you know, this tastes different—I mean really different—to other stuff.* I wonder if there was something in the air in 1908, and I think about my grandmother—a young, working-class woman from Lancashire—lost in the endless chatter of a rattling mill, licking her lips one morning, and perhaps thinking: *yes, this is of itself—neither sweet nor sour, neither salty nor bitter. There will be wars, disasters, and horrors unimaginable in the city where I shall raise my daughter, and in the city where she will, in turn, raise children of her own. Yet this, now, here on my tongue, is the twentieth century, with all its dreams of flight.*

That it took the span of two World Wars, The Beatles, Feminism, Stonewall, Snoopy, and Live Aid to decide that mushrooms tasted of mushrooms and nothing else—even as some nourished us, some made us very sick indeed, and some filled our heads with pulsing synaesthetic light—clearly says more about what it was to savour that century of change than any chemical analysis.[2] For instance, while umami may be precisely defined as 'the taste of salts combining glutamate, inosinate or guanylate with the likes of sodium ions, such as monosodium glutamate, or potassium ions', where in this description is the knees-up 'round the pub piano,[3] the decimation of British industry,[4] or Freddie leading 'the note heard round the world'?[5]

Which leads me on to the second point which particularly fascinates me. *Sweet, sour, salty,* and *bitter*: all familiar tastes, yet all wrapped up in different words, depending upon the tongue wrapped around it. I say *sweet,* you say солодкий (*solodkyy*)—let's call the whole thing 甘い (*amai*). But umami is umami, every time it's tasted or spoken. Accents aside, no one is claiming it for their own yet, as if we're still surprised by this thing that we all tasted but which no one noticed, and for which we still haven't found our own words.

This is where these poems arise: the things which have always been distinct but never noticed; the things which haven't found words that are really our own yet; the things I was told not to put in my mouth but did anyway. Some nourish me, some make me very sick indeed, and some fill my head with pulsing synaesthetic light.

Notes

1. The symposium program may be found on the Society for the Research on Umami Taste's website at https://www.srut.org/acten/714/. The Society's website was an invaluable resource in approaching the subject.

2. Other cultural references are available.

3. A once popular phenomenon which fell out of favour in the mid-century due to changes in popular entertainment (and technology). As David Huckvale notes, for instance, Terence Fisher's 1952 film *Stolen Face* could utilise this trope when a concert pianist entertains drinkers in a country pub with more popular fare after initially drawing from their usual repertoire, though the practice was by then on the wane (Huckvale, David 2022 *The Piano on Film*, Jefferson, NC: McFarland, 30).

4. See, for example, the following: Tomlinson, Jim 2021 'Deindustrialisation and "Thatcherism": Moral Economy and Unintended Consequences', *Contemporary British History* 35:4, 620–42; and the website at https://www.bbc.co.uk/news/uk-england-lincolnshire-61625497. Also consider the taste, like rage or despair, which is distinct but does not yet have a name.

5. Can you remember what you were doing on 13 July 1985? Can you remember what it tasted like?

PAUL HETHERINGTON

Sourness, in its innumerable varieties, is one of the most extraordinary flavours the world offers. It is also persistent in evolutionary terms, being able to be tasted by a wide variety of species that do not have the capacity to appreciate some of the other tastes. Rob Dunn comments that 'all the species that have been tested [about 60 so far] are able to detect acidity in their food', and he also remarks that '[s]our taste was likely present in ancient fish' (2021, n.p.), crucially enabling them to sense the acidity of the water they encountered. Part of the reason that sourness is so widely recognised may be because of the various health benefits associated with sour foods. These benefits differ between different species, but include the capacity to help in the absorption of iron, anti-inflammatory properties, the capacity to boost the immune system and de-toxifying effects.

Whether it is the calamansi, the kumquat, the grapefruit, the lime, or the lemon, tart citrus fruits are perhaps the most well-known purveyors of sourness in the mouth. Tamarind is also famous for its astringency, complemented in the ripe fruit by a beguiling sweetness. Other fruits, such as cherries and rhubarb, are also well-known for a sourness that is combined with sweetness—although, in the case of rhubarb the sweetness is mainly provided by adding sugar or other fruit, such as apple, during the cooking process.

Vinegar is also famously sour, as are some wines, sour beers, sour liqueurs and sour cocktails. There are sour candies, such as Warheads or Toxic Waste; the sour and spicy kimchi; sourdough bread; salty and sour Japanese plums (or umeboshi); and various sour pickles. There are sour gooseberries, sour yoghurt and sauerkraut. Some of these flavours are the result of processes of fermentation, which Dunn has speculated may have been crucial to human development:

> Our ancestors would have chosen to ferment fruits or roots because the result was pleasurable. But they would have benefited from doing so because the result was also nutritious. Fermentation makes calories more available ... It also adds some nutrients to food ... [and it] became a way of storing food ...[that] could be eaten during the leanest of seasons. (2022, 168)

The list of sour foods I have mentioned could be vastly extended, indicating that sour flavours are an intrinsic part of human experience. As a result, they are often referred to metaphorically—perhaps most famously in Aesop's fable about the fox and the sour grapes. Sourness in Aesop's story represents frustration and disappointment, and the word is also used to refer to other human feelings and sentiments, including disillusionment, resentment, irritability and fretfulness. Language's capacity to express sourness especially interests me, as does the sour dissonance of some music. I am also interested in the sour aspects of recollection and of history itself. Despite history's many accounts of heroism and advancement, it is underpinned by repeated instances of warfare, violent colonisation and associated atrocities.

Indeed, one form of sourness may be considered part of almost all human experience—the kind of sour realism that runs counter to naïvely saccharine, romanticised or idealised views of humanity. Repeated human encounters almost inevitably engender some degree of sourness which, in turn, adds piquancy and pleasure to subsequent sweet feelings—just as sour flavours in food often enhance the honeyed flavours they contain. Sourness may not often be pleasant in itself but, when combined with the world's multifarious flavours— whether these are understood literally or metaphorically—it is an important, even essential, part of the pleasures of eating, living, reflecting, creating and being.

Works Cited

Dunn, Rob and Monica Sanchez 2021 *Delicious: The Evolution of Flavor and How It Made Us Human*, Princeton, NJ: Princeton University Press

Joosse, Tess and Rob Dunn 2022 'Pucker up! Why Humans Evolved a Taste for Sour Foods', *Science*, 11 February, https://www.science.org/content/article/pucker-why-humans-evolved-taste-sour-foods

PAUL MUNDEN

Somewhat against the grain of other prose poetry practice, I have sought, in this new sequence, to avoid the 'traditional' solid block of text, feeling the need to allow for a greater variation in rhythmic structure. Perhaps the concept of 'sweetness and light' made me take the decision to let some air into the poems, to excuse them from that breathlessness— I might even say claustrophobia—that is a feature of much prose poetry. My chosen model is that of Geoffrey Hill's *Mercian Hymns*, a book of prose poems consisting of what Hill calls versets, a term typically relating to the psalms. Each verset may consist of one or more prose sentences (or fragmented sentences). I have also followed Hill's choice of layout, with the body of each verset hanging indented from the first line. This, again, distinguishes each 'block' from the more customary paragraph, and adds further space and light.

In my previous chapbook within this shared series, I tackled the Iron Age, the grimmest of all Hesiod's notional eras, and I instantly opted for Sweet from the range of tastes explored in this new set; I wanted some light relief! But having found Hesiod's horrors in such close relation to our twenty-first century, I have it seems struggled to escape the darker currents of human dealings in these 'sweet' poems. Fairy tales are in the mix, but of course those tend to have a dark core too. The pandemic that we have lived through no doubt also contributed to the darkness, though again, the impulse was to escape, and the progression of my sequence, structured in three parts, does at least attempt to leave the darkness behind. There is, I hope, a strong element of humour helping out.

I mention 'sweetness and light', something of a cliché, and part of my purpose has been to interrogate the range of cliché associated with the concept and word: sweet. It is frequently coupled with an extraordinary range of other words and phrases, nowhere more so than in popular song. Having been immersed in writing about music over the past year or so, both in prose and poetry, it was perhaps inevitable that music and song should in any case feature here; musical references stacked up pretty quickly. But another principal influence has been the work of the late Pete Morgan, a friend and fellow poet whose lines I borrow for the opening epigraph. The phrase 'sweet voices' is yet another musical allusion but it also, in Pete's poem, refers to the speaker's enemies. It's a beguiling idea, and one that encapsulates the contradictory forces at large in my sequence.

Works Cited

Hill, Geoffrey 1971 *Mercian Hymns*, London: André Deutsch

Morgan, Pete 1973 *The Grey Mare Being the Better Steed*, London: Secker & Warburg

✳

JEN WEBB

The term 'bitter' gets bad press; as though all that is bitter is wrong, tastes wrong, does wrong. In fact, bitter has its own rich qualities, its own affordances for human life. For example, while all children are more sensitive to bitter than are adults, those more sensitive to its flavour are also less likely to be obese. The active ingredients that give food and medicines their power do on the whole taste bitter (Mennella et al., 2013), but in exchange they offer healing and wellbeing.

Bitterness is the most complex and the most sensitive of the tastes, presumably because so many toxic substances are also bitter (Drewnowski, 2001). But while this taste alerts humans to the possible presence of poison, it is equally present in chocolate, caffeine, salt, sweeteners; and it significantly enhances the flavour of many foods. 'Bitterness is a double-edged sword', writes chef Jennifer McLagan. 'It signals toxic and dangerous, but it can also be pleasurable and beneficial ... Eschewing bitter is like cooking without salt, or eating without looking' (2014, n.p.). We think we don't like bitter tastes—a hangover perhaps from childhood—yet olives, walnuts, white asparagus, citrus peel, craft beer, salad greens, radicchio, Campari, and Brussels sprouts all delight many adults.

Knowing this, still we preserve the name 'bitterness' for those things we dread, or resist, or reject: the bitter truth, bitter weather, bitter love, bitter memory. In these poems I am trying to incorporate the complexity of the taste, and the gentler, more accommodating aspects of bitter/ness; trying to explore the discourse that swirls around the flavour, and maybe infuse it with an aftertaste of honey.

Works Cited

Mennella, Julie A., Alan C. Spector, Danielle R. Reed and Susan E. Coldwell 2013 'The Bad Taste of Medicines: Overview of Basic Research on Bitter Taste', *Clinical Therapeutics* 35:8, 1225–246

Drewnowski, Adam 2001 'The Science and Complexity of Bitter Taste', *Nutrition Reviews* 59:6, 163–69

McLagan, Jennifer 2014 *Bitter: A Taste of the World's Most Dangerous Flavor*, Berkeley, CA: Ten Speed Press

ABOUT THE POETS

Cassandra Atherton is an award-winning writer and scholar of prose poetry. She was a Visiting Scholar in English at Harvard University and a Visiting Fellow in Literature at Sophia University, Tokyo. Her most recent books of prose poetry are *Leftovers* (Gazebo Books, 2020) and the co-written *Fugitive Letters* (Recent Work Press, 2020). She has written extensively on the atomic bomb, both critically and creatively and is currently working on a book of prose poetry on the Hiroshima maidens with funding from the Australia Council. With Paul Hetherington, Cassandra co-wrote *Prose Poetry: An Introduction* (Princeton University Press, 2020) and co-edited the *Anthology of Australian Prose Poetry* (Melbourne University Press, 2020). She is co-host of the international poetry livestream reading series, *LitBalm* and associate editor at MadHat Press (USA). ✰

Oz Hardwick is a European poet, photographer, occasional musician, and accidental academic, whose work has been widely published in international journals and anthologies. He has published eleven full collections and chapbooks, including *Learning to Have Lost* (IPSI, 2018) which won the 2019 Rubery International Book Award for poetry, and most recently *A Census of Preconceptions* (SurVision, 2022). Currently he is as excited as a teenager about the debut album *Paradox Paradigm* by his international/interdimensional space rock collective Space Druids. Oz is Professor of Creative Writing at Leeds Trinity University. Who'd have thought it? www.ozhardwick.co.uk ◎

Paul Hetherington is a distinguished Australian poet. He has published seventeen full-length collections of poetry and prose poetry, including *Ragged Disclosures* (Recent Work Press, 2022), *Her One Hundred and Seven Words* (MadHat Press, 2021) and the co-authored epistolary prose poetry sequence, *Fugitive Letters* (with Cassandra Atherton; Recent Work Press, 2020). He has also edited nine further volumes. He has won or been nominated for more than thirty national and international awards and competitions, recently winning the 2021 Bruce Dawe National Poetry Prize. Paul is Professor of Writing in the Faculty of Arts and Design at the University of Canberra where he is head of International Poetry Studies (IPSI). ✺

Paul Munden is a poet, editor and screenwriter living in North Yorkshire. A Gregory Award winner, he has published six poetry collections, the latest of which is *Amplitude* (Recent Work Press, 2022). He was director of the UK's National Association of Writers in Education, 1994–2018, and is now a Royal Literary Fund Fellow at the University of Leeds. He is also an Adjunct Associate Professor at the University of Canberra, Australia, where he established the Poetry on the Move festival. ✺

Jen Webb is Dean of Graduate Research at the University of Canberra, and co-editor of the scholarly journal *Axon: Creative Explorations* and the literary journal, *Meniscus*. She researches creativity and culture, and recent publications include *Art and Human Rights: Contemporary Asian Contexts* (with Caroline Turner; Manchester UP, 2016), and *Gender and the Creative Labour Market* (with Scott Brook et al., Springer, 2022). With Paul Hetherington she is co-editor of the bilingual (Mandarin/English) anthology *Open Windows: Contemporary Australian Poetry* (Shanghai Joint Publishing Company, 2016). Her recent poetry collections are *Moving Targets* (Recent Work Press, 2018) and, with Shé Hawke, *Flight Mode* (Recent Work Press, 2020). ✳

IPSI: INTERNATIONAL POETRY STUDIES

International Poetry Studies (IPSI) is part of the Centre for Creative and Cultural Research, Faculty of Arts and Design, University of Canberra. IPSI conducts research related to poetry, and publishes and promulgates the outcomes of this research internationally. It also publishes poetry and interviews with poets, as well as related material, from around the world. Publication of such material takes place in IPSI's online journal *Axon: Creative Explorations* (www.axonjournal. com.au) and through other publishing vehicles. IPSI's goals include working—collaboratively, where possible—for the appreciation and understanding of poetry, poetic language and the cultural and social significance of poetry. IPSI also organises festivals, symposia, seminars, readings and other poetry related activities and events.

CCCR: CENTRE FOR CREATIVE AND CULTURAL RESEARCH

The Centre for Creative and Cultural Research (CCCR) is IPSI's umbrella organisation and brings together staff, adjuncts, research students and visiting fellows who work on key challenges within the cultural sector and creative field. A central feature of its research concerns the effects of digitisation and globalisation on cultural producers, whether individuals, communities or organisations.

CPSIA information can be obtained
at www.ICGtesting.com
Printed in the USA
BVHW010500101222
653842BV00023B/1588